A Jataka Tale

Come Back, O Tiger!

Kindness to Animals and Respect for the Earth Series

Instilling Goodness Books

Buddhist Text Translation Society

Come Back, O Tiger!

Published by: Buddhist Text Translation Society
Copyright © 2013 by Buddhist Text Translation Society

All rights reserved. No part of this book may be reproduced in any form or by any electronic or mechanical means including information storage and retrieval systems without permission in writing from the publisher.

Dharma Realm Buddhist University
Dharma Realm Buddhist Association

Retold by Bhikshuni Jin Rou
Illustrations by Christy Whitworth
Design by Laura Tan

Come Back, O Tiger! is a story retold of one of the Buddha's earlier lifetimes, with ecological implications. The original tale is The Little Tree Spirit, No. 272, in the Pali Jataka collection.

Library of Congress Cataloging-in-Publication Data

Jin Rou, Bhikshuni.
 Come back, o tiger! : a Jataka tale / retold by Bhikshuni Jin Rou ; illustrations by Christy Whitworth.
    pages cm. – (Kindness to animals and respect for the earth series)
  ISBN 978-1-60103-015-3
 1. Tipitaka. Suttapitaka. Khuddakanikaya. Jataka. Vyagghajataka–Paraphrases–Juvenile literature. 2. Jataka stories, English–Juvenile literature.
 I. Whitworth, Christy, illustrator. II. Tipitaka. Suttapitaka. Khuddakanikaya. Jataka. Vyagghajataka. III. Title.

BQ1470.V8822E55 2012
294.3'82325–dc23

2012012477

Come back, o tiger to the woods again,
Let it not be leveled with the plain.
For, without you, the ax will lay it low;
You, without it, forever homeless go.
—Jataka Tales

This story of kindness and compassion is a Jataka tale that the Buddha told his followers about one of his innumerable past lives.

In this tale the Buddha appears as a wise tree spirit to teach that all beings are a living part of the earth. Only by developing empathy with each other and all of earth's creatures, can we protect the environment.

In order to teach this higher truth about life, the tale has been retold in simple language for children to easily understand.

A hot day slowly came to an end as the bright orange sun began to slide behind a forest in India. Lizards scuttled about and slipped into the cracks of an old cassia tree. A large Bengal tiger stretched and yawned after a nap under the shade. He rolled over and slowly got to his feet. He had not eaten in days and was hungry.

Hearing something move behind the bushes, he crouched on a rock and waited. A bristly-haired boar ran out. With a quick spring, the tiger pounced. The boar was fast, but the tiger was faster.

As a bright moon appeared in the sky, the tiger dragged his prey under the old cassia tree and settled in for an evening feast.

After he ate his fill, he hid the remains under a bush. The next day the putrid smell from the rotting carcass rose up with the morning mist, permeating the forest air.

High in the branches of the old cassia tree lived a purple tree spirit who was very foolish. Next to it was a beautiful young cassia tree where a wise, green tree spirit lived. The tree spirits had been friends forever, playing happily together among the yellow blossoms, sipping their sweet nectar.

The foolish spirit awakened as the first ray of sun touched the top of her tree. "Pew! What's that smell?" she asked.

The wise spirit peeked down. "It's our friend, the tiger," she said, blinking sleepily.

"He's not my friend!" said the foolish spirit. "He stinks. And look at the mess he's making. The air is no longer fresh and clean. I'm getting rid of that beast!"

"Please don't!" begged the wise spirit. "The balance of life in this forest depends on that very tiger."

"But just imagine how pure the air will be, I must do it!"

The tiger returned at dusk to gnaw on the bones. Teetering on a branch above him was the foolish spirit. Just then a strong breeze blew through the forest. "Ah, here is my chance!" she said and shook her tree with all her might. "O-o-o-o!" she moaned like a scary ghost.

Blossoms flew wildly in the air. "It's a ghost!" roared the tiger. "This forest is haunted!" Filled with terror he fled, never to return.

The wise spirit said, "You shouldn't have scared off the tiger, you will see why."

Years passed. Peace and quiet reigned in the forgotten forest. The tiger's pugmarks washed away and the piles of bones turned into rich earth. The foolish spirit played the time away, while the wise spirit watched and waited.

One day a cow came thrashing through the forest, with a young boy running after it. "Come back" the boy yelled. "The tiger will eat you."

The boy stopped and listened. He remembered stories that the villagers had told about the tiger that lived in the forest and how they dare not go into its depths. As he proceeded slowly, he looked around for signs of the tiger, but saw none--no scattered bones, no claw scratches on the tree bark, and no pugmarks.

He only heard the sound of rustling leaves under his feet and the cry of a wild peacock. It seemed as if the tiger had never lived there. So the boy rested in the shade and made chains of marigolds while the cow grazed on the sweet green grass. "It's so peaceful here and the air is fresh and clean," he said. "This would be a good place to live."

The next day the boy brought his father to the forest, who agreed this would be a wonderful place to live. His father cut down some trees and built a house by the river. Others came and the forest was soon full of people.

They plucked the fruit and trampled down the flowers and grass. They cut down the trees to build houses and to make land for farms. The smoke from their fires choked the forest. Heaps of garbage piled up under the trees.

The hubbub never stopped. People chattered and quarreled, pigs squealed, and dogs barked. The wise spirit was worried. "The forest is in trouble," she said.

The foolish spirit was at her wits end. "Hey! Hey! Stop that racket!" she shouted at the people. "Can't a tree spirit get some peace and quiet? And clean up that stinking rubbish!"

One day the foolish spirit looked down in surprise. Two men with axes flung over their shoulders walked toward her tree. She smiled and said, "I can frighten those men away the same way I did that tiger." And she shook the tree with all her might and moaned in a ghostly howl, "O-o-o-o!"

Blossoms flew wildly in the air. "Watch out!' cried the short man. "The tree is haunted."

"Nonsense," the tall man said, looking up at the tree. "It's only the wind blowing, This tree will make good firewood. Let's cut it down."

"Did you hear what he said?" the foolish spirit cried fearfully, "I should have listened to you, my little friend. Please help me!"

The wise spirit shook her head. "There's nothing I can do now," she said sadly. "I'm afraid it's too late."

One man swung his ax. Suddenly an idea, a way to save her friend, came to the wise spirit. "It might just be possible," she said, "I'll try it." And she opened her little mouth as wide as she could and out came the fiercest tiger roar she could muster. "Roar-r-r-r-r!"

"Tiger! Run!" cried the men and they ran away as fast as their legs would carry them.

"You saved the life of my tree and me too!" said the foolish spirit in her joy. "Because of my foolishness, the forest is being destroyed. I must find that tiger and apologize, and invite him back to the forest before it's too late."

And so it was, balance was returned to the forest. The tree spirits lived out the lives of their trees until they all grew old and returned to the earth. Now new trees grow with different tree spirits living in them, continuing the cycle of the forest, as it should be.

Not long ago, the tigers almost faded away. People hunted them for their coats and for medicine, and sold them to circuses and zoos. They cut down the forests, so the tigers had no place to live and no food to eat. Now the people are stopping and they say, "Just a minute. The forest had lots of tigers, now there aren't many. Maybe we should stop cutting down the trees and replant them. We should clean up the rivers and lakes too."

It is taking a while, but many people are working together to rescue the forests before it's too late. Trees are being planted and land is set aside for wildlife to roam freely again. What would life be like without trees and squirrels and butterflies? If we can save the tiger, we can save the earth.

Ten ways to help save the forest and creatures who live in it.

1. Recycle paper and buy recycled products.
2. Use cloth napkins and towels.
3. Cut down on trash; don't eat junk food!
4. Eat less meat. Better yet, eat a plant-based diet. It takes land the size of a small kitchen for just one hamburger.
5. It's best not to buy things made from fur or leather, turtle shell, feathers, ivory, or bones.
6. Avoid using products that are tested on animals or contain chemicals that pollute rivers and kill fish.
7. Use less gasoline and plastic. They are made of oil that may come from rainforests.
8. Stop going to circuses and marine parks, where animals are held captive. Read books and watch movies about nature, instead.
9. Photograph wild flowers and enjoy their beauty forever. Plucking them needlessly is destructive.
10. Write to your government representatives to let them know that you oppose any operations that may harm wildlife or wildlife habitat.

Help the rangers find and rescue the tiger cub before it is too late!

Reproducible page. Draw on the back and recycle.

Instilling Goodness Books

Come Back, O Tiger!
Human Roots, Buddhist Stories
No Words--Teachings of the Buddha
The Awakened One (English and Chinese)
The Giant Turtle (English, Spanish, Chinese)
The Legend of Mahaduta (English, Spanish)
The Light of Hope (English and Chinese)
The Spider Thread (English and Chinese)
Under the Bodhi Tree
The Kind Monk

Berkeley Series

Kindness
Dew Drops
Meditation Handbook
Whole Body-Vegan Lifestyle

To order books, please visit: bttsonline.org or write to:
City of 10,000 Buddhas, 4951 Bodhi Way, Ukiah, CA 95482

The City of Ten Thousand Buddhas is a spiritual community founded by Venerable Hsuan Hau. It is the home of Dharma Realm Buddhist University, Instilling Goodness Elementary and Developing Virtue High Schools. Our doors are open to people from any country who wish to devote themselves to the pursuit of humaneness, justice, and ethics. Families and children are especially welcome to attend our schools and programs.

www.drba.org / www.drbachinese.org
Information about schools or summer camp: www.igdvs.org